W9-CEG-226

THE ELEMENTS

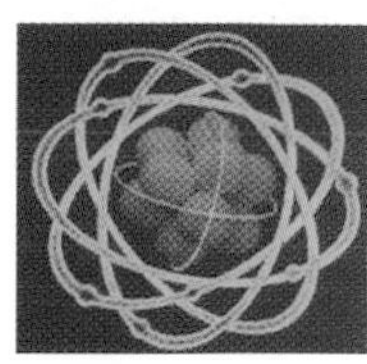

Magnesium

Colin Uttley

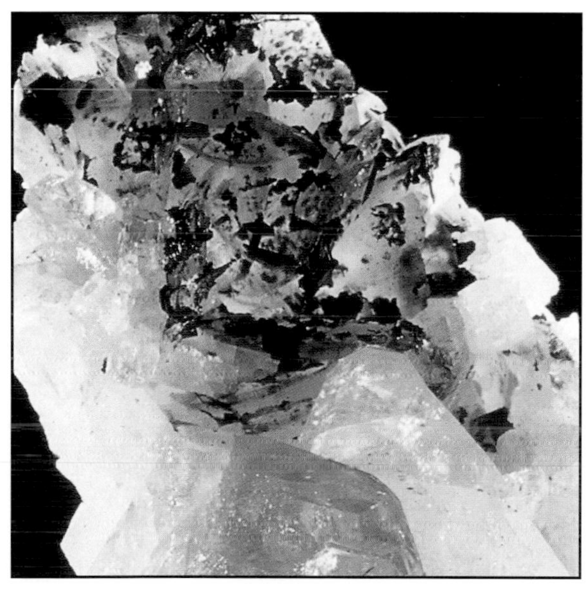

BENCHMARK BOOKS

MARSHALL CAVENDISH
NEW YORK

Benchmark Books
Marshall Cavendish Corporation
99 White Plains Road
Tarrytown, New York 10591-9001

Library of Congress Cataloging-in-Publication Data
Uttley, Colin.
Magnesium / Colin Uttley.
p. cm. — (The elements)
Includes index.
Summary: Explores the history of the bright-colored metal magnesium and explains its chemistry, how it reacts, its uses, and its importance in our lives.
ISBN 0-7614-0889-4 (lib. bdg.)
1. Magnesium—Juvenile literature. [1. Magnesium.] I. Title.
II. Series: Elements (Benchmark Books)
QD181.M4U77 2000
546'.392—dc21 98-53200 CIP AC

Printed in Hong Kong

Picture credits
Corbis (UK) Ltd: 15, 16, 18, 20, 23, 24, 25, 26, 30.
Image Bank: 4, 14, 17, 22.
Image Select: 7, 12.
John Bates: 13.
Science Photo Library: 9, 10, 21, 27.
TRH Pictures: 19.

Series created by Brown Packaging Partworks
Designed by wda

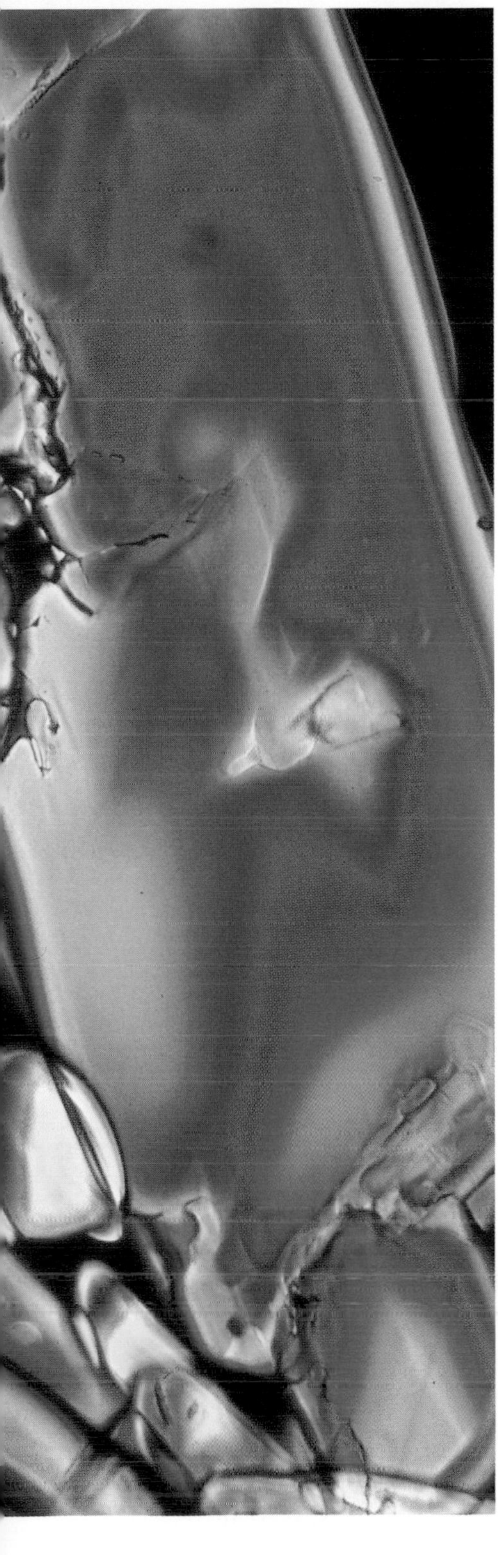

Contents

What is magnesium?

Magnesium is used in steelmaking factories, such as this one, to improve the purity of the steel.

Magnesium is a silvery white metal valued throughout the world because of its light weight. Of all the metals used to make structural components, magnesium is the lightest—about 66 percent of the weight of aluminum and just 25 percent of the weight of steel.

Magnesium is solid at room temperature. It is 1.74 times denser than water. In other words, one cubic meter of magnesium weighs 1.74 times more than one cubic meter of water. Magnesium melts at 1,200°F (651°C), when it can be poured into molds to make objects. It turns into a gas at 2,025°F (1,107°C), which is important in one of its extraction processes.

Magnesium is never found naturally in its pure state, as a metal, since it readily reacts with other elements to form compounds.

Magnesium and the periodic table

Magnesium is in Group II of the periodic table, among the other elements, such as calcium and barium, called alkaline-earth metals. Magnesium has the chemical symbol "Mg."

Inside the atom

Magnesium, like every other element, is made up of tiny particles called atoms. Each atom contains even smaller particles: protons, electrons, and neutrons. Protons have a positive charge, electrons are negatively charged, and neutrons are neutral, which means they have no charge. Magnesium has atomic number 12. This means that the nucleus at the center of each magnesium atom contains 12 protons. An atom has the same number of electrons as protons, so each magnesium atom has 12 electrons. The electrons circle the nucleus in layers called electron shells.

Magnesium atoms come in three varieties, called isotopes, which differ in the number of neutrons they have. Isotopes behave in exactly the same way chemically, but they have different atomic masses. Seventy-nine percent of magnesium atoms have an atomic mass of 24—that is, they have 12 neutrons and 12 protons in their nucleus. Ten percent have 13 neutrons and an atomic mass of 25. Eleven percent have 14 neutrons and an atomic mass of 26. Magnesium has an average atomic mass of 24.31.

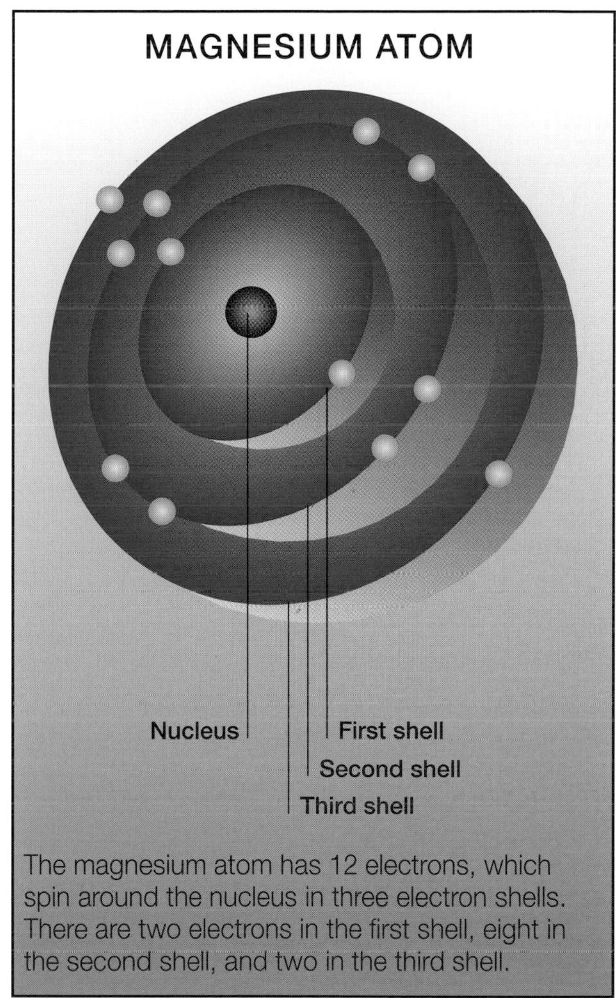

The magnesium atom has 12 electrons, which spin around the nucleus in three electron shells. There are two electrons in the first shell, eight in the second shell, and two in the third shell.

Good reactions

Magnesium is important in steelmaking. A major problem in steelmaking is the presence of sulfur. The main constituent of steel is iron, and this element reacts with sulfur. This reduces the quality of the steel, so the sulfur has to be removed. Magnesium is more reactive than iron, so when magnesium powder is added to the molten steel, the sulfur reacts with magnesium rather than with the iron.

Gray matter

Magnesium's reactivity can be a problem. Magnesium objects can corrode, as the metal reacts with small impurities of iron and nickel left over from refining. Today, the refining process is much improved, and magnesium is less likely to corrode.

New magnesium objects quickly discolor, as moisture in the air reacts with the magnesium to form a coating of magnesium oxide, which then protects the metal beneath from further corrosion.

Special properties

Magnesium in its pure form is a bright-colored metal. It is highly reactive, which means that it readily combines with other elements to form a large number of compounds, many of which have commercial and domestic uses.

For example, magnesium reacts readily with the oxygen in air to form magnesium oxide. The oxide covers the bright metal as a dull gray film, or tarnish. Corrosion like this is a relatively slow process. A faster, more spectacular way of producing magnesium oxide is to heat a piece of magnesium in a flame, when the metal burns with a brilliant white light.

Magnesium also reacts readily with steam from boiling water to form magnesium oxide. Magnesium reacts with cold water, too, but the reaction is much slower than it is with steam. The products of the reaction are also different. Instead of combining only with the oxygen atoms in water to form magnesium oxide, the magnesium reacts with one of the hydrogen atoms too, forming magnesium hydroxide, which has the chemical formula $Mg(OH)_2$. The most familar form of this magnesium compound is as the cloudy solution known as "milk of magnesia," which has a variety of medicinal uses.

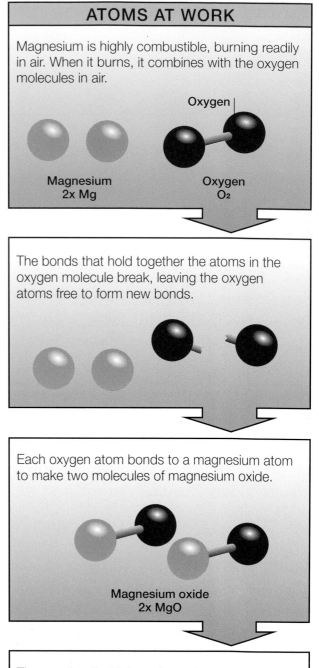

ATOMS AT WORK

Magnesium is highly combustible, burning readily in air. When it burns, it combines with the oxygen molecules in air.

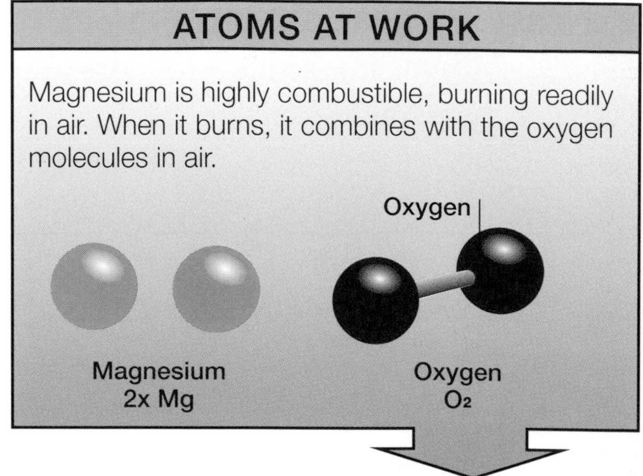

The bonds that hold together the atoms in the oxygen molecule break, leaving the oxygen atoms free to form new bonds.

Each oxygen atom bonds to a magnesium atom to make two molecules of magnesium oxide.

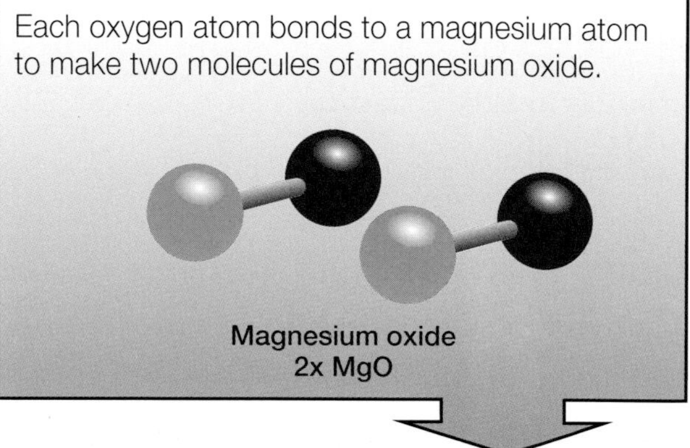

The reaction that takes place when magnesium reacts with oxygen can be written like this:

$$2Mg + O_2 \rightarrow 2MgO$$

This shows that two atoms of magnesium react with the two atoms in a molecule of oxygen to form two molecules of magnesium oxide.

In the early days of photography, magnesium was used to create dramatic flashlights.

A bright idea

Early photographers made good use of magnesium. The photographic plates in their cameras needed a lot of light to produce good pictures. Sometimes the camera shutter had to stay open for many minutes, which was fine for a still life or landscape, but a problem for portraits.

Photographers saw that magnesium filings burn easily with a bright, white light and soon realized how this could solve their problems. Magnesium filings were mixed with potash (potassium chloride) and spread along a holder called a pan. When the shutter was opened, the mixture was ignited, flooding the scene with enough bright light to get a clear image in a fraction of a second. This technique also gave us a new expression—"a flash in the pan"—meaning anything that comes and goes quickly.

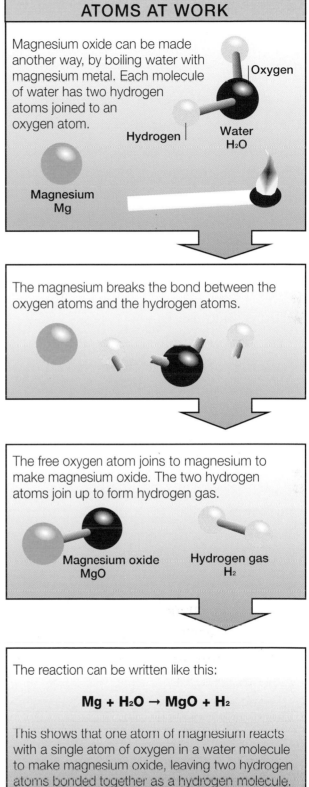

ATOMS AT WORK

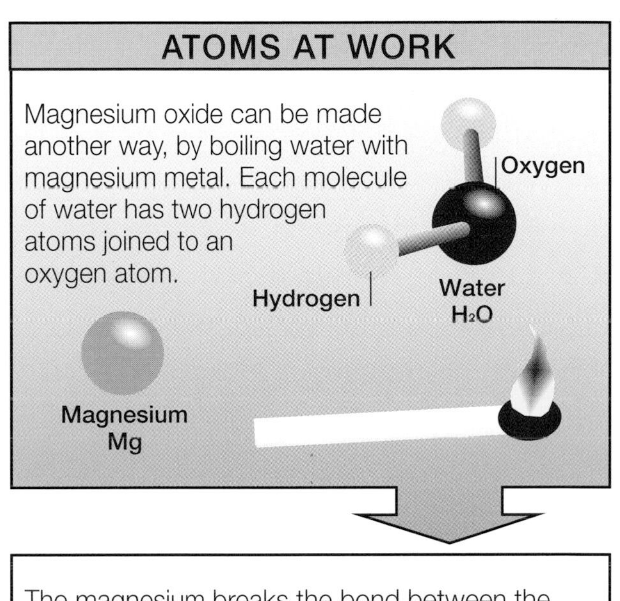

Magnesium oxide can be made another way, by boiling water with magnesium metal. Each molecule of water has two hydrogen atoms joined to an oxygen atom.

The magnesium breaks the bond between the oxygen atoms and the hydrogen atoms.

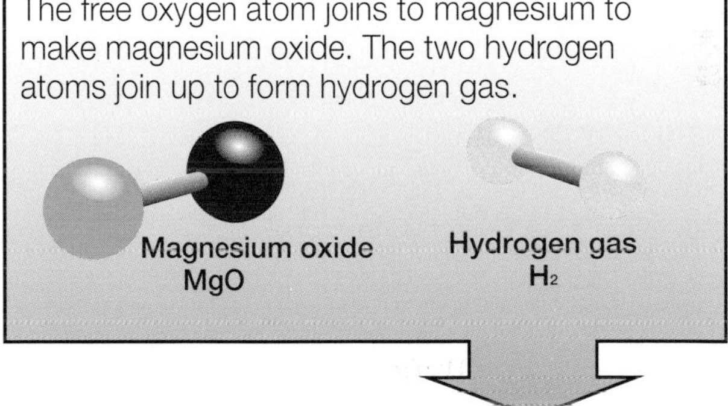

The free oxygen atom joins to magnesium to make magnesium oxide. The two hydrogen atoms join up to form hydrogen gas.

The reaction can be written like this:

$$Mg + H_2O \rightarrow MgO + H_2$$

This shows that one atom of magnesium reacts with a single atom of oxygen in a water molecule to make magnesium oxide, leaving two hydrogen atoms bonded together as a hydrogen molecule.

Compounds of magnesium

Magnesium is so reactive because the two electrons in the outermost shell of the magnesium atom are easily lost. When an atom gains or loses an electron, it forms an ion. Ions, which carry a positive or negative electrical charge, try to join up with other, oppositely charged ions in order to restore the electrical balance that the atom—with its equal number of electrons and protons—has.

The magnesium ion, having lost two electrons, has a positive charge of two and is described by the symbol Mg^{2+}. Being positive, magnesium ions are strongly attracted by negative ions, such as sulfate (SO_4^{2-}), carbonate (CO_3^{2-}), and chloride (Cl^-) ions, to form what are known as ionic compounds.

Magnesium reacts rapidly with dilute acids to form what are called salts of

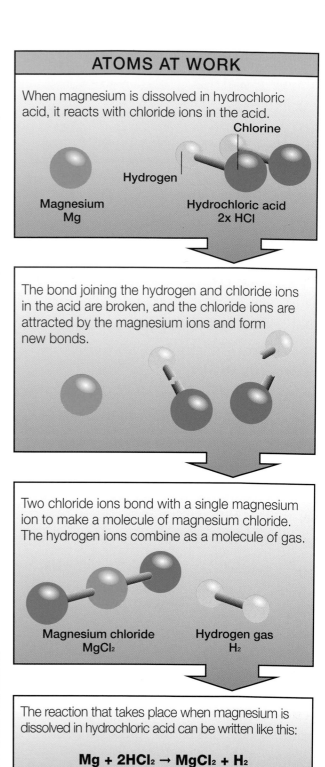

DID YOU KNOW?

USEFUL MAGNESIUM COMPOUNDS

Magnesite, or magnesium carbonate, is used to make inks, glass, rubber, pharmaceuticals, and food additives. It is also used as insulation for boilers and pipes.

Magnesium chloride is used to make tough cements for flooring and in the textile industry.

ATOMS AT WORK

When magnesium is dissolved in hydrochloric acid, it reacts with chloride ions in the acid.

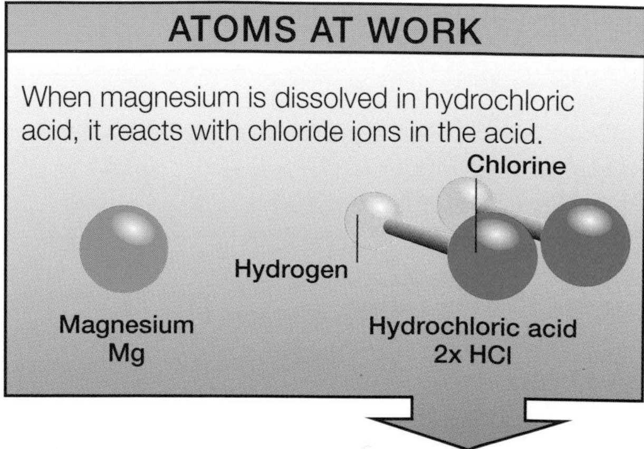

The bond joining the hydrogen and chloride ions in the acid are broken, and the chloride ions are attracted by the magnesium ions and form new bonds.

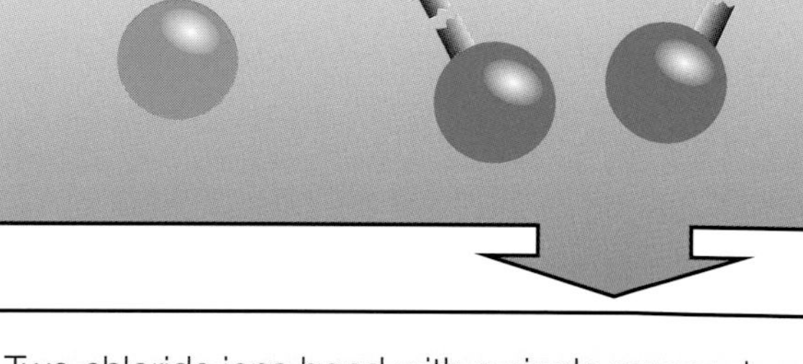

Two chloride ions bond with a single magnesium ion to make a molecule of magnesium chloride. The hydrogen ions combine as a molecule of gas.

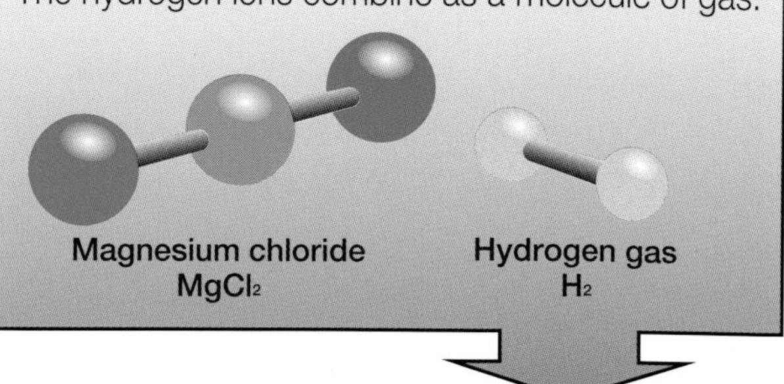

The reaction that takes place when magnesium is dissolved in hydrochloric acid can be written like this:

$$Mg + 2HCl_2 \rightarrow MgCl_2 + H_2$$

This shows that one atom of magnesium reacts with two molecules of hydrochloric acid to make one molecule of magnesium chloride and one molecule of hydrogen.

magnesium. For example, it reacts with hydrochloric acid to form magnesium chloride, and with sulfuric acid to form magnesium sulfate.

Magnesium metal is made by electrolyzing magnesium chloride, while the uses of magnesium sulfate include fireproofing and leather-processing.

A soft touch

Next time you have a bath, would you think of dusting your body with hydrated magnesium silicate? You might when you realize that its more familiar name is talc. This magnesium compound is not just used as a cosmetic; it is also an essential material in the manufacture of paper, plastic, and paint.

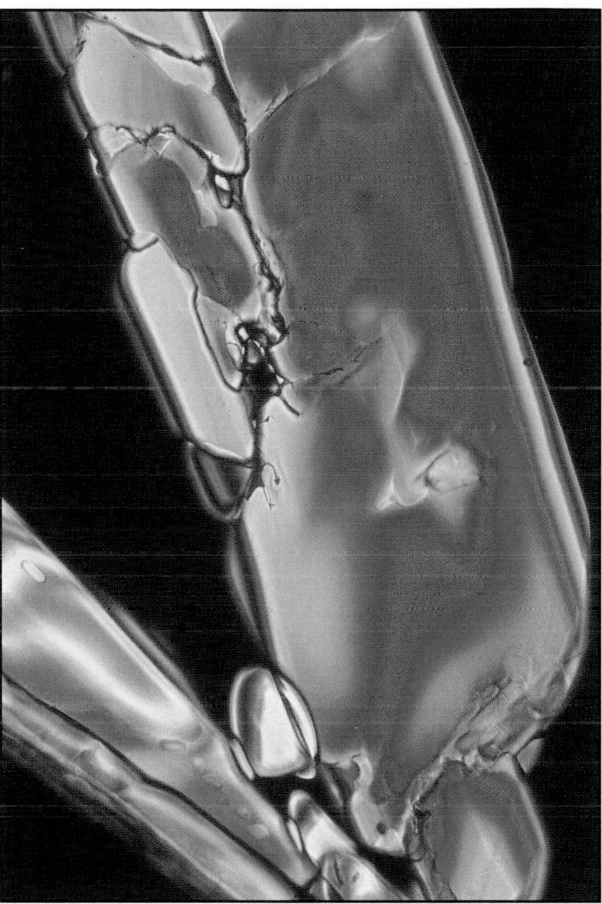

These are crystals of magnesium sulfate seen through a powerful microscope. Magnesium sulfate is used in the textile industry and has various medicinal uses.

DID YOU KNOW?

SMOOTH OPERATOR

One of the reasons talc is so useful is that it is the softest material there is. The hardness of minerals is measured on a scale called the Mohs' scale. The hardest material, diamond, measures 10 on this scale, but talc measures just one. Talc is so soft because of the way its atoms are joined together. Layers of brucite (magnesium joined to oxygen and water) are sandwiched in between layers of silica (silicon bonded to oxygen). The layers of brucite and silica are only very weakly attached. This means that if they are pushed, the weak bonds break and the layers easily slide over each other.

A fine read

Without talc, this book might look very different. Paper is made from the fibers of trees that have been cut and mashed up to produce a pulp. The fibers are tightly compressed when the paper is rolled, but there are still tiny gaps left between the fibers. Talc is used to fill these gaps and make the paper white and smooth. Another effect the talc has is to stop the ink from smudging on the page.

Where magnesium is found

There is a lot of magnesium in the world—in fact, about 2.5 percent of Earth is made of magnesium. Because magnesium combines so easily with other elements, it never occurs as pure metal. To get magnesium that we can use, we have to separate it from other elements.

The two main sources of magnesium are in naturally occurring minerals, or ores, called dolomite and magnesite. Magnesite is a mixture of carbon, oxygen, and magnesium. Dolomite is a mixture of calcium, carbon, oxygen, and magnesium. Both ores are mined all over the world.

DID YOU KNOW?

A DROP IN THE OCEAN

Seawater is full of magnesium. Every 2.2 lbs. (1 kg) of seawater contains about one-twentieth of an ounce (1.2 grams) of magnesium. That might not seem like a lot, but it means that if you could take the magnesium from one cubic kilometer of seawater, it would weigh 1.18 million tons (1.06 million tonnes).

Magnesium from either ore

There are two ways to get the magnesium out of the ore. If the ore is heated to about 2,910°F (1,600°C), the magnesium turns into a gas that can be pumped away. When the gas cools down, it first turns into liquid and then into solid magnesium.

The other method is electrolysis. This uses an electrical current to separate magnesium from its ore. At 1,290°F (700°C) the ore turns to liquid. Two rods (electrodes), made of different materials, are placed into the mixture. As the current flows between them, the various chemicals in the

The white crystals in this rock sample are dolomite, and the pink crystals are apatite. Both dolomite and apatite are minerals that contain magnesium.

ore separate, and the magnesium is attracted to one of the rods.

Seawater contains a high proportion of magnesium ions, making the oceans a rich and valuable source of magnesium.

The first step in extracting magnesium from seawater is to get the magnesium ions dissolved in the water to settle out as an insoluble solid, called a precipitate. This is done by adding lime (calcium oxide) to the seawater, which produces a precipitate of magnesium hydroxide. The precipitate is filtered out of the water and then mixed with hydrochloric acid. This reaction produces magnesium chloride, which is melted and electrolyzed.

DID YOU KNOW?

OUT OF THIS WORLD

One day, there might be another place to get magnesium—space. The asteroid belt is a part of our solar system between Mars and Jupiter and is made up of hundreds of thousands of pieces of rock. Some are very small, but others are as large as 625 miles (1,000 km) across. Asteroids are made from many different materials, including iron and diamond, and some contain as much as 12 percent magnesium. Some scientists are planning to capture asteroids and put them into orbit around Earth. If they succeed, these orbiting asteroids could be mined for valuable minerals. It would be very expensive to do this today but, in the future, as we use up more and more of the supplies on Earth, we could be forced to look beyond our planet for magnesium.

ATOMS AT WORK

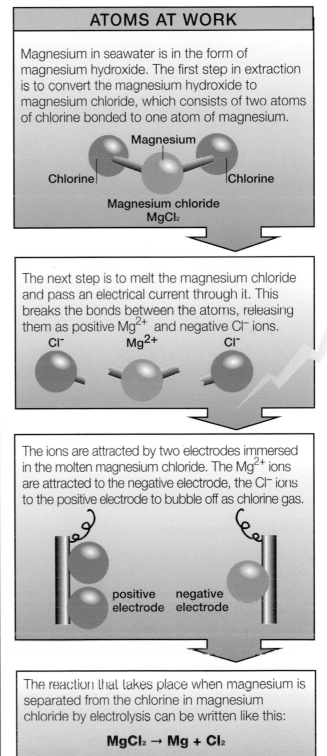

Magnesium in seawater is in the form of magnesium hydroxide. The first step in extraction is to convert the magnesium hydroxide to magnesium chloride, which consists of two atoms of chlorine bonded to one atom of magnesium.

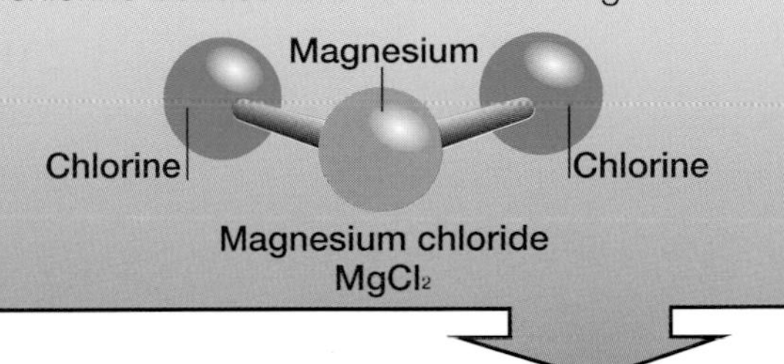

The next step is to melt the magnesium chloride and pass an electrical current through it. This breaks the bonds between the atoms, releasing them as positive Mg^{2+} and negative Cl^- ions.

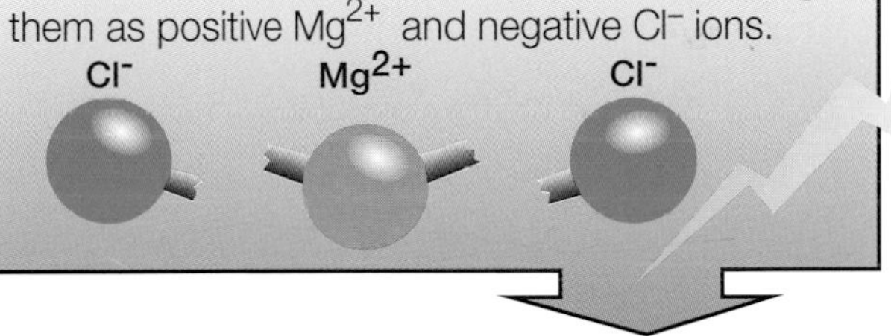

The ions are attracted by two electrodes immersed in the molten magnesium chloride. The Mg^{2+} ions are attracted to the negative electrode, the Cl^- ions to the positive electrode to bubble off as chlorine gas.

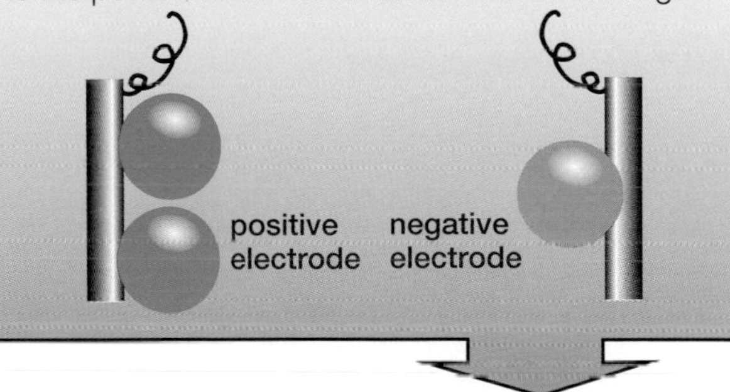

The reaction that takes place when magnesium is separated from the chlorine in magnesium chloride by electrolysis can be written like this:

$$MgCl_2 \rightarrow Mg + Cl_2$$

This shows that a magnesium chloride molecule is broken down into a magnesium atom and two chlorine atoms bonded together as a molecule.

How magnesium was discovered

The person who discovered magnesium could not have done it without help—from his cows. In 1618, a farmer in Epsom, England, had trouble getting his cattle to drink from his well. The water had a bitter taste that the cows did not like. Luckily, the farmer noticed that when the water splashed on the cows' bodies it helped scratches and rashes to heal. The water, named Epsom salts, soon became popular as a cure for almost all ailments.

The chemical that had given the water its bitter taste was magnesium sulfate, which is a compound of three elements: magnesium, sulfur, and oxygen. Over thousands of years, the action of rain on the surrounding rocks had caused the magnesium sulfate to dissolve out of the rock into the well water.

The famous British chemist Sir Humphry Davy (1778–1829) was the first person who managed to isolate pure magnesium.

> **DID YOU KNOW?**
>
> ***SIR HUMPHRY DAVY***
>
> Sir Humphry Davy is best remembered for inventing the Davy lamp, a lamp that could burn in coalmines without causing explosions. But he was an intrepid experimenter who made many discoveries. As well as making pure magnesium, he also isolated several other elements, including sodium and potassium. He would investigate gases by breathing them in, and he once nearly died when he inhaled water gas—a poisonous mix of hydrogen and carbon monoxide.
>
> Sir Humphry Davy helped to found London Zoo and, toward the end of his life, retired from active science to write a book on fly-fishing.

A star turn

Because magnesium joins very easily to other chemicals, it is never found by itself in nature. It was nearly 200 years after the discovery of Epsom salts before anyone managed to make pure magnesium. The person who did that was British scientist Sir Humphry Davy (1778–1829).

DID YOU KNOW?

EPSOM SALTS

Epsom salts are still used today for medicinal purposes. They are also used in the tanning and dyeing industries, as well as the manufacture of fertilizers and cements.

At the end of the 18th century, a number of wealthy men had taken an interest in science, or "natural philosophy," as they called it. They decided to pay for a building in London that would serve as a center for research and a meeting place for people interested in science. The Royal Institution, as it came to be called, had laboratories, a library, meeting rooms, and a lecture theater.

The Royal Institution soon became a very fashionable place to visit, and the most popular events were talks by the Director of the Institution, Humphry Davy. In fact, so many people wanted to hear him talk that Albermarle Street, where the Royal Institution was, became blocked by their horse-drawn carriages. To keep the traffic flowing, the world's first one-way street was introduced.

DID YOU KNOW?

HOW MAGNESIUM GOT ITS NAME

The name *magnesium* comes from Magnesia, an area of Greece that has deposits of magnesium ore. The ore is found throughout the world and magnesium is very common, making up about 2.5 percent of Earth's crust.

Davy in his element

Sir Humphry Davy was a remarkable scientist. In 1807, he became the first person to isolate the elements sodium and potassium. The following year, in 1808, Davy mixed together two chemicals—magnesium oxide and mercuric oxide—and passed an electric current through the mixture. The effect was to make the magnesium separate out from the oxide as pure metal. Davy wanted to call his new discovery "magnium," but it later became known as magnesium.

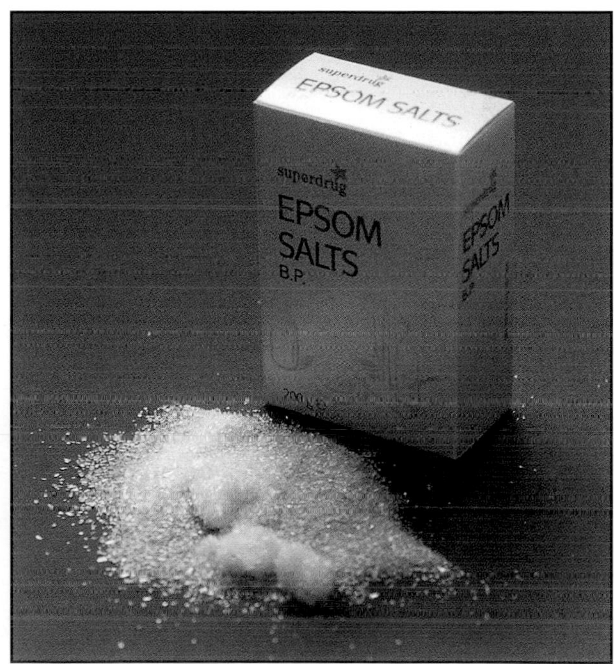

Crystals of magnesium sulfate, commonly called Epsom salts.

Magnesium alloys

Most of the magnesium objects described in this book are not quite what they seem. They nearly all contain small amounts of other metals.

Mix and match

For years, metallurgists (scientists who study metals) have been concocting recipes to improve metals. Just a small amount of another metal can make a huge difference to the finished product by changing one or more of its properties. It can make the material stronger, or easier to work with, or less likely to corrode. These mixtures of metals are called alloys.

Magnesium would not be so useful if it was not for the other metals that are added to it. Aluminum is the metal most usually added to magnesium. An alloy of 9 percent magnesium and 9 percent aluminum is more than twice as strong as magnesium alone. Adding 3 percent aluminum and one percent zinc makes an alloy that can be pulled into shape without cracking, and just 0.2 percent of the metal manganese produces an alloy that will not corrode.

We usually think of cans such as these, which have been crushed during the process of recycling, as being made of aluminum. In fact, they are not made of pure aluminum but of aluminum mixed with small amounts of magnesium.

Different combinations of silicon, zirconium, and even silver can also be added to magnesium to make just the right alloy for every job.

Casting thousands

There are many different ways to make things from magnesium. It can be hammered, rolled, carved, or pulled into shape. But the most common way of shaping magnesium is the casting process.

In casting, molten metal is poured into a mold and allowed to cool down. This is sometimes done in the traditional way, using sand. First, a model of the shape that is needed is made out of wood or metal. This is called a pattern. The pattern is used to make an impression in a bed of fine sand that has been mixed with oil so that it keeps its shape. Once the impression has been made, the pattern is removed and liquid magnesium is poured into the sand to take on the shape left by the pattern.

Most magnesium objects are made using a technique called die casting. In this method of mass production, the first step is to make a special kind of mold made of two parts called dies. Molten magnesium is then pumped at high pressure into the gap between the two dies. The space between the dies is in the shape of the thing that is being made. When the magnesium has cooled to a solid, the two dies are pulled apart and the finished object is taken out.

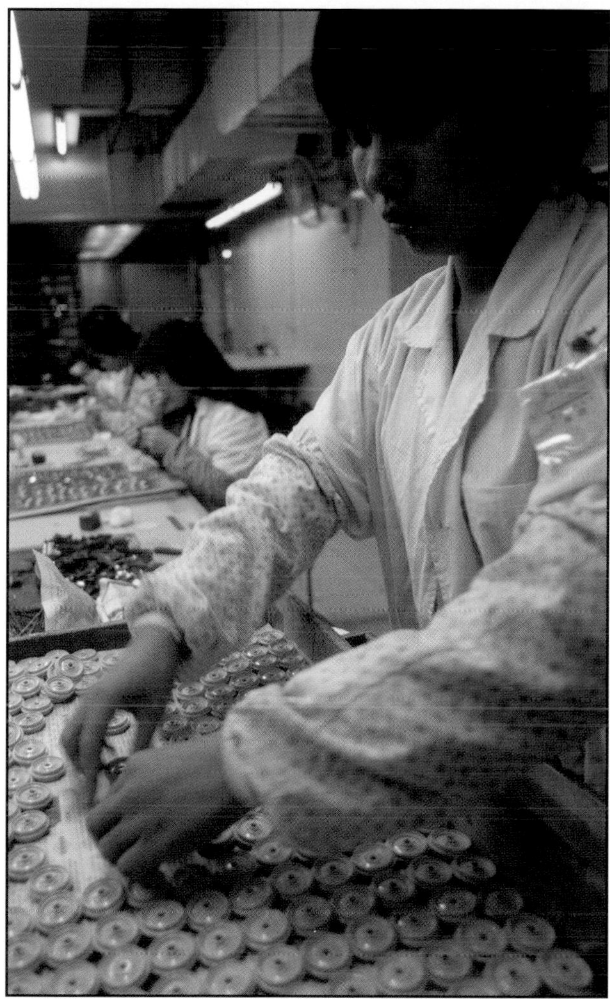

Die casting, being used here to make large numbers of identical tractor parts, is a simple way to mass produce certain metal goods. A high proportion of the objects made from magnesium alloys are manufactured by this process.

MAGNESIUM FACTS

IN THE CAN

Drink cans are usually made from aluminum alloys that contain some magnesium—1.5 percent in the body of the can and 4.5 percent in the top. If empty cans are recycled, the magnesium can be extracted and reused.

Light work

Most of the magnesium extracted from ore is not used to make pure magnesium products. About half of all the magnesium made is mixed with aluminum to make alloys. Most things made from aluminum also contain some magnesium.

Although magnesium has been around in pure form since 1808, its large-scale use only began in the mid-20th century, when people started to use magnesium alloys in the manufacture of high-performance aircraft and automobiles.

Today magnesium is used to make thousands of everyday objects, such as bicycle frames, camera bodies, archery bows, lawn mowers, and computer frames.

Wobbly wheels

In the 1950s, the designers of race cars were in a race of their own—trying to beat the competition.

Cars take corners best when their tires spend as much time as possible in contact with the road, giving maximum grip. That, and not comfort, is the main reason why automobiles have springs. The big problem for race-car designers is that heavy wheels and tires do not make very efficient use of the springs. The wheels tend to bounce up and down a lot before the

Lightweight alloys made from magnesium are used in modern race-car design. That is because in motor racing weight is of vital importance—each extra ounce slows the car down and could mean the difference between winning and losing.

These bicycle frames are made from two of the lightest metals—magnesium and aluminum.

springs are able to bring them under control. This is because the heavier an object is, the harder it is to stop it moving.

The solution to the problem was to make the wheels even lighter by using a magnesium alloy. To give the wheels extra strength, they were designed with a wobbly, rather than the usual flat, shape and were popularly called "wobbly web" wheels. Modern race cars still use wheels made from magnesium alloy, but the wobbly shape has gone now.

Photoengraving

Magnesium alloy is also used in printing, in a process called photoengraving. In this process, plates of magnesium alloy are covered in a light-sensitive coating. A photographic negative is placed over the coating, and the whole thing is exposed to ultraviolet light. Exposed parts of the coating harden, but the parts shielded from light by the negative stay soft. The soft areas are washed away, leaving bare metal. The metal plate is dipped in acid, which eats away exposed areas only. Then the covering is stripped off, ink is rolled on to the plate and copies are printed off.

The innovative Volkswagen Beetle was the first automobile to make extensive use of magnesium. At the time, in the 1930s, engines were usually made from a far heavier metal—iron. The Beetle had an engine entirely built from magnesium.

On the road

For many years, magnesium had been used to make such automobile components as steering columns, instrument panels, and gearbox casings. But now it is being used for bigger parts, with some prototype automobiles having the whole body made from magnesium.

New rules, especially in the United States, have forced motor manufacturers to build cars that burn less fuel. A good way to meet the new regulations is to make cars that are very light, because the lighter a car is, the less fuel it needs to move it along. Magnesium is the lightest metal in common use, so it is ideal for the latest, lightweight automobiles.

The electric automobiles now being introduced in some cities need heavy batteries to power their motors. Here too, magnesium is used to reduce weight and allow drivers to go further before they have to stop to recharge the battery.

Skid stuff

A Formula One race car will throw out a trail of very bright sparks as it speeds along the racetrack at 190 mph (300 kph). Race cars are designed to run as close to the ground as possible—to reduce the amount of air resistance, or drag—and they work best when they are just skimming the road surface. Magnesium skid plates are used to protect the underside of the car and stop it from being damaged. As the magnesium rubs along the ground, it gets very hot and parts of it begin to burn, throwing out showers of sparks that look very dramatic. But this is what is meant to happen—because it is the replaceable skid plate, not the car, that is being worn away.

Today, computers are invaluable tools in automobile design. But magnesium and its alloys are just as vital in motor manufacture, being used to make a variety of components—from wheels to batteries, gearboxes to skid plates.

DID YOU KNOW?

IRONING OUT THE BUGS

In the 1930s, German automobile designer Dr. Ferdinand Porsche (1875–1951) was not afraid to try something new when he built his newest creation, which was later to become the most successful automobile there has ever been—the Volkswagen Beetle. Porsche knew about the advantages of magnesium, and he knew that by keeping the automobile's weight down, it would be cheaper to run. So, he built the whole of the engine block—the main body of the engine—from magnesium. If Porsche had used iron, as most motor companies did at that time, his new car would have been 130 lbs. (60 kg) heavier, just because of that one part.

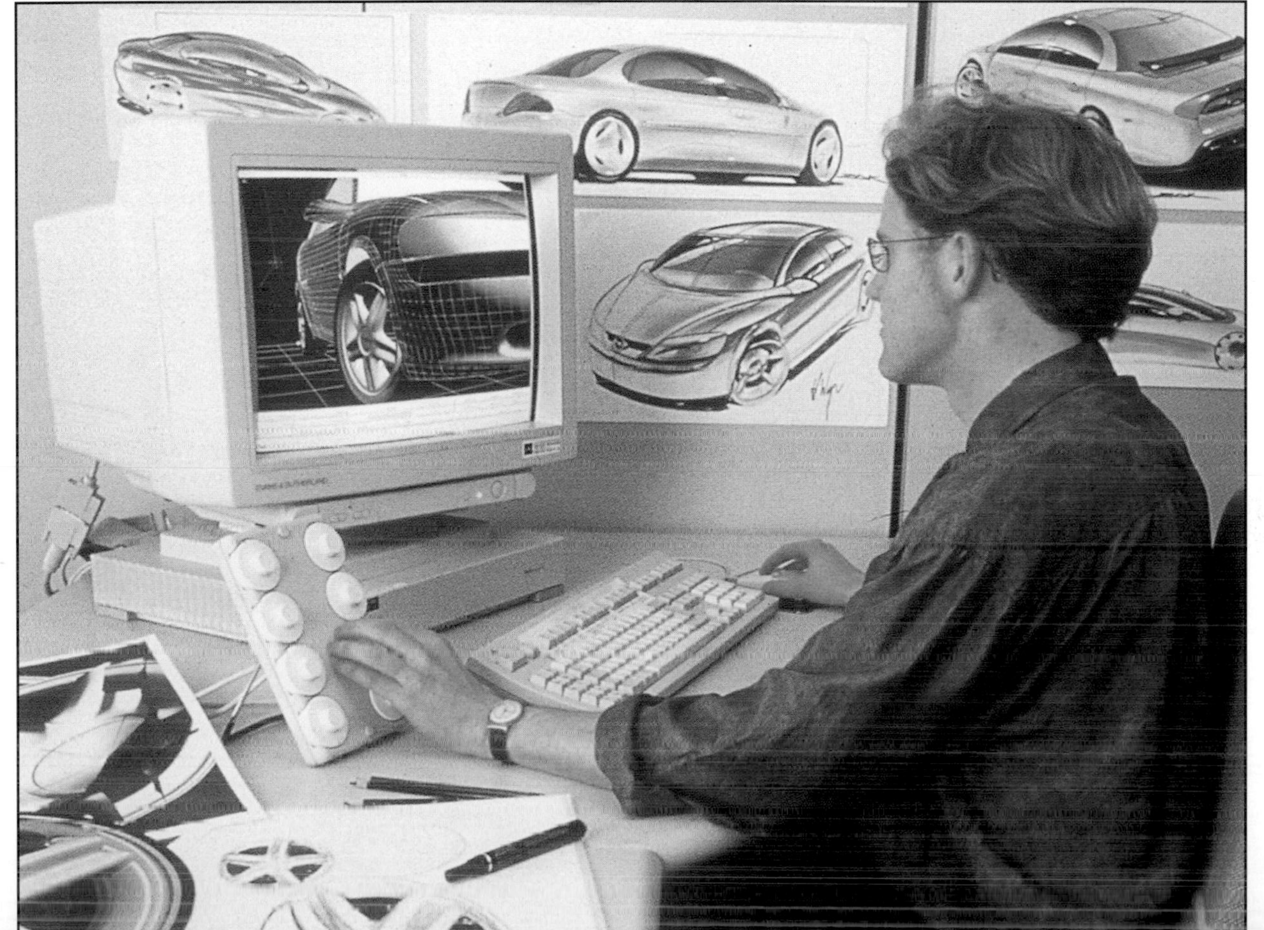

Up, up, and away

Designers of aircraft and rockets are always looking at ways to keep the weight down. Every pound that is trimmed from their designs allows an extra pound of fuel or cargo to take its place.

Losing weight

Magnesium is used to keep down the weight of jet engines. Although it cannot stand temperatures in the hottest parts of the engine, magnesium is used to make the large casing into which all the other components are fitted. The magnesium casing from the engine of a jumbo jet is about 7 ft. (2 m) across.

Heavy decisions

You might wonder why, if magnesium is so light, whole aircraft are not made from it. However, designers have to look at other properties besides lightness in deciding which materials to choose. For some uses, a component made from magnesium would not be practical. For example, aluminum is heavier than magnesium, but it is also stronger. So, in some components, if aluminum were replaced by magnesium, the component would be heavier because it would need to use that much more magnesium to achieve the same strength as the aluminum.

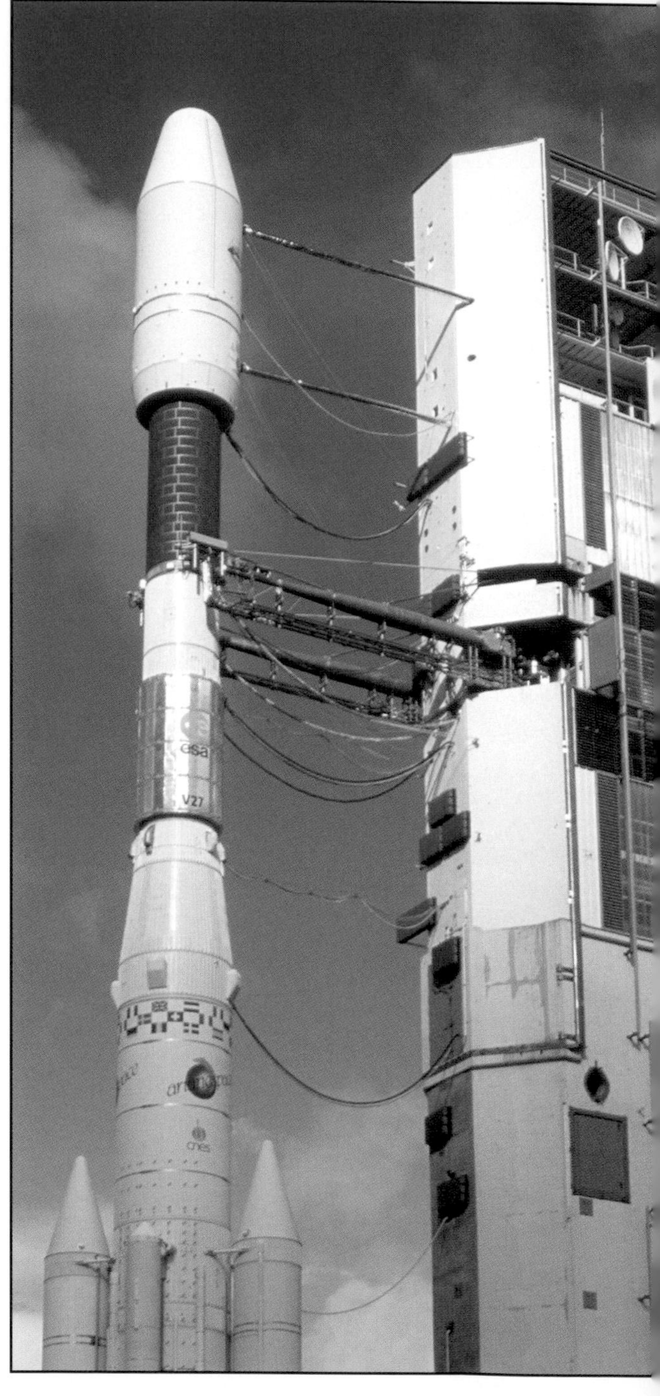

Although not the most heat-resistant of elements, magnesium can still withstand considerable temperatures. This, as well as its lightness, makes it suitable for use in the manufacture of various components for rockets such as Ariane 4 *above.*

Another thing that has to be considered is the way the material would react with any other materials around it. For example, placing magnesium next to components made of steel could lead to serious corrosion of the steel.

Yet another problem is temperature. For example, titanium is a metal used in the parts of jet engines where temperatures are highest. Though it is heavier than magnesium, titanium can withstand temperatures 1,800°F (1,000°C) greater than magnesium can before it melts.

DID YOU KNOW?

SPACE SAVINGS

Weight-saving is especially important when it comes to space flight. The cost of putting a satellite into space is $45,000 for each pound ($100,000 per kilogram). Magnesium alloy is used in making both the interiors and exteriors of rocket boosters. It is used to make fins, parts of the motor, and small components such as camera housings and equipment containers.

Carbon copier

These days, a new material is rivaling magnesium in air and spacecraft construction. Carbon fiber is strong and light and, because it is built up layer by layer, it can be tailor-made for any application with exactly the right strength in the right place.

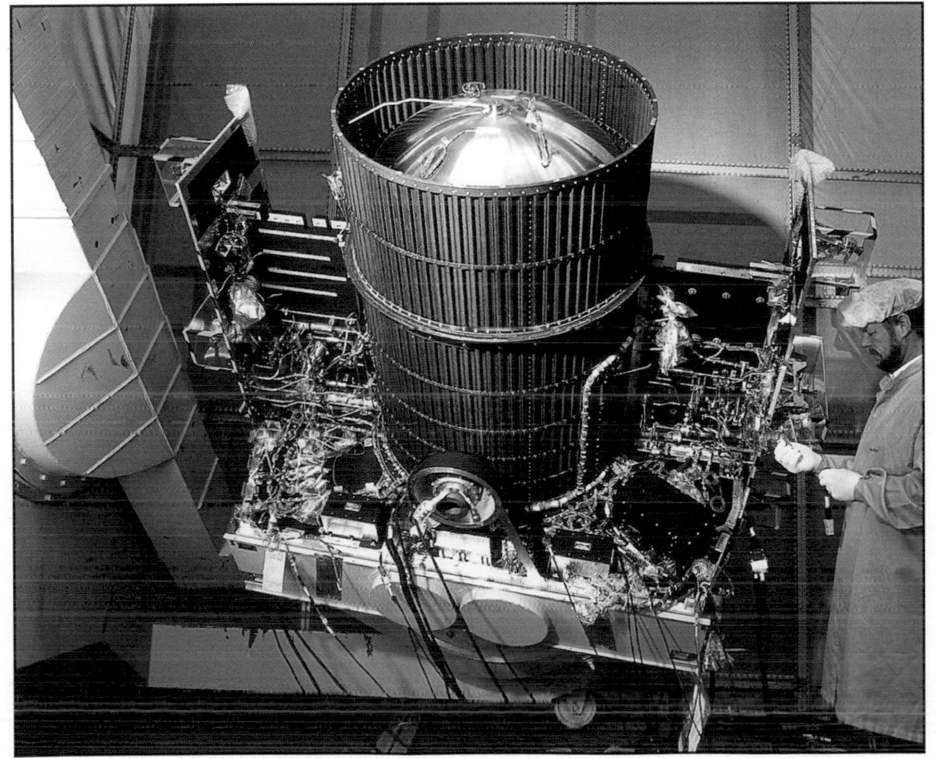

A key consideration in building and launching communications satellites is weight. Each component that is heavier than it needs to be adds to the launch costs. Magnesium's relatively low atomic mass makes it both a very useful weight saver and a vital money saver.

Fire power

Fireworks have been used for centuries, but in the 19th century new chemicals were used to make them brighter and more colorful than ever. Magnesium was first tried in fireworks in 1865. Packets of fine magnesium powder were packed in rockets, to make them burn with a brilliant white light. Aluminum, sodium, strontium, copper, iron, and many other elements were used to make a rainbow of colors that are still used today.

Star attractions

Magnesium is not just used to make bright fireworks—it can make noisy ones too. The loud crackling or sizzling noise made by some fireworks is the result of mixing magnesium with aluminum. Some rockets contain large balls of magnesium powder arranged to make giant star shapes that will burn for many seconds.

Magnesium, with its brilliant white light, is an essential ingredient of most modern fireworks. This Fourth of July display would be a lot less exciting without magnesium.

Not all the uses of magnesium are peaceful. This highly reactive and potentially explosive element is used in the manufacture of a range of military hardware.

The light and the dark

For many years, audiences at firework displays the world over have been thrilled by the intense light and loud crackling of burning magnesium. Sadly, there is a darker side to this story of colorful explosive power. The same spectacular properties of magnesium have been used to make weapons of war. These include incendiary bombs, which are designed to start fires, and tracer bullets, which help military personnel to see the direction of machine-gun fire. So, magnesium can be the cause of both wonder and wounds.

On the roof

During World War II, fire watchers were stationed on rooftops across London, England. Their job was to locate incendiary bombs dropped from the air by German bombers and to put them out—hopefully before they did much harm. But there was a problem with the equipment they had. The stirrup-pump that sprayed water on to the bombs actually made them burn more strongly, because the water reacted with the magnesium. A far safer way to put out an incendiary bomb was to cover it with sand.

A good friend

Magnesium has so many uses, but they are not all as obvious as fireworks, automobiles, and airplanes. For example, magnesium can help to warm our homes and save us from the sea.

Magnesium power

Magnesium is essential to many nuclear power plants. The reactor, the part of the plant that makes heat, uses uranium as a fuel. Uranium—one of the heaviest elements on Earth—produces heat when its atoms break apart. Such elements are called "radioactive," and they can be very harmful to living things they come into contact with. Magnesium helps to keep the radioactive material inside the reactor. At the same time, it lets out the heat, which makes steam to drive the turbines that make the electricity.

Magnesium is the only material that can do this difficult job. Other materials would melt, corrode, burst, or soak up most of the atomic particles that are needed to make the reactor work.

Magnesium is important in ensuring the safety of nuclear reactors such as this one in France.

Life jackets such as these often include an emergency battery partly made from magnesium.

Just add water

Magnesium can be used to make an emergency battery for use at sea. A battery needs three components to work: two electrodes (one positive and one negative, each of a different material) and a liquid (called an electrolyte) that surrounds the electrodes. The battery works as electrons move from one electrode to the other.

In an emergency battery, the electrodes are made from magnesium and silver chloride. The electrolyte is the seawater surrounding the survivor. Survivors simply pour seawater into the battery, and they have a power source for an emergency radio. Small versions are fitted to life jackets so that as soon as they hit the water, the battery begins to work, powering a light that could bring rescue.

Stopping the rust

Seawater contains dissolved oxygen ions that attack metals, especially reactive ones, and cause corrosion. In the case of oil rigs, supertankers, and underwater pipes, this can be a serious cause for concern as the iron in the steel pipes, oil-rig supports, and tanker hulls turn to rust.

Placing magnesium next to the steel can prevent such rusting. To understand how it does this, think back to the emergency battery. Again, seawater acts as the electrolyte and magnesium as the positive electrode (also called an anode). The iron in the steel is the negative electrode.

As an electrical current flows between the electrodes, oxygen ions are attracted most strongly by the more reactive magnesium. The magnesium is attacked, rather than the less reactive iron, and the magnesium corrodes instead of the steel. For this reason, the magnesium is often called a sacrificial anode.

Magnesium in living things

Magnesium is essential for all living things. It is found in every plant and animal. In fact, magnesium makes up 0.00027 percent of your body.

The heart of the matter

A lack of magnesium in the body has been linked to an increased risk of heart attacks. Magnesium and calcium work together in our muscles to help them move. Without these elements, our muscles would not work properly. Calcium helps muscles to contract (shorten) and magnesium helps them to relax. To pump blood around the body, heart muscles must contract and relax more than once a second throughout our lives. Magnesium deficiency can stop heart muscles from relaxing properly and trigger a heart attack.

In some areas, water from the faucet is said to be "hard," meaning that it contains mineral deposits that include magnesium and calcium. Areas with "soft" water have fewer of these deposits. Statistics show that people living in hard-water areas are, on

This woman is carrying giant magnesium tablets to be displayed as part of an exhibition in the 1930s. Fortunately, the magnesium tablets that people take are much smaller!

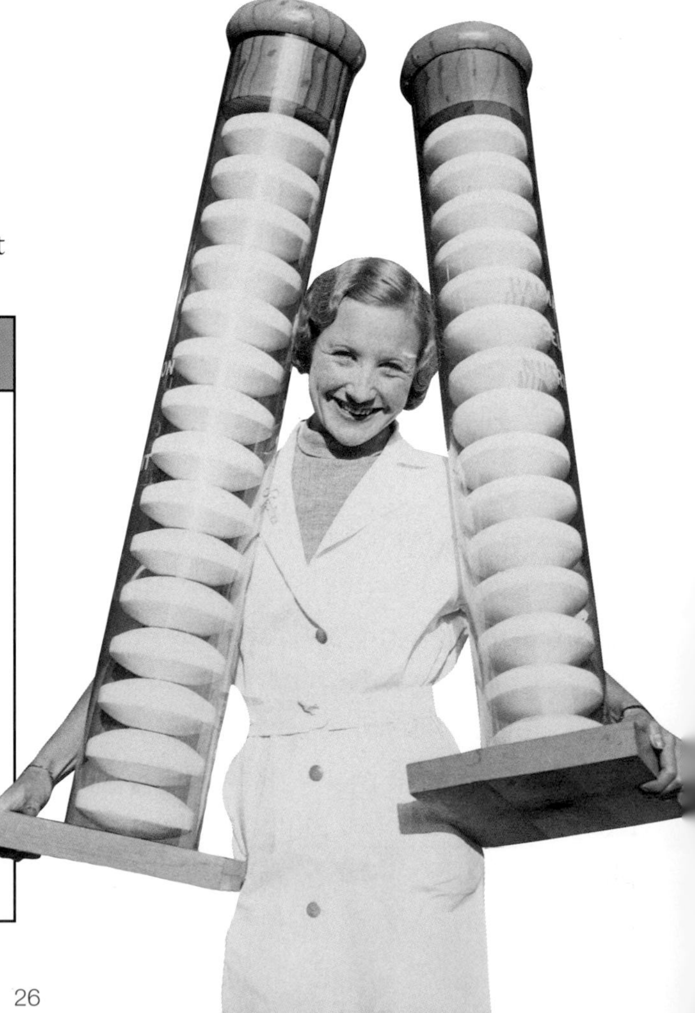

DID YOU KNOW?

GOING TOO FAR

Although magnesium is vitally important to health, some doctors are worried that some people are overdoing it. These people take large quantities of antacid or laxative drugs, many of which contain magnesium. Older people are most at risk because their bodies cannot get rid of excess magnesium as easily as younger people. Taking excess magnesium can cause vomiting and breathing problems. It is estimated that magnesium "overdoses" have caused 14 deaths in the United States in the last 30 years.

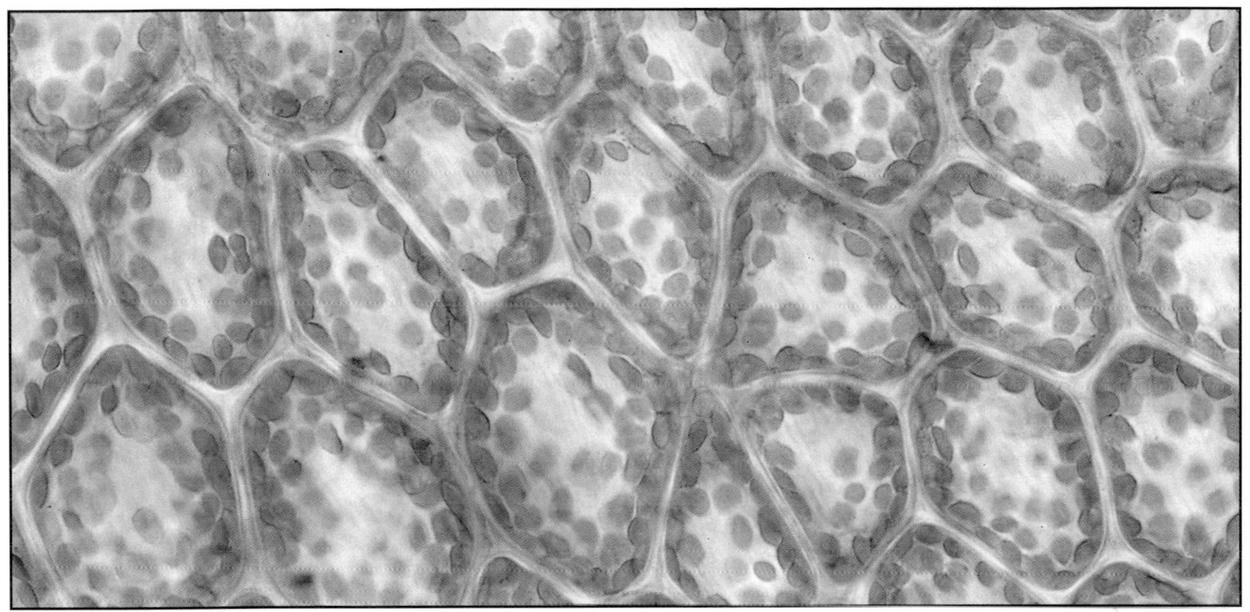

Chlorophyll is the chemical that enables green plants to absorb sunlight to produce food in the process called photosynthesis. Chlorophyll, shown here in magnified plant cells, contains magnesium.

DID YOU KNOW?

IN THE MEDICINE CABINET

Magnesium hydroxide, or milk of magnesia, is not only used in the production of magnesium metal. It is also used as a laxative and as an antacid to treat indigestion.

DID YOU KNOW?

BONING UP ON MAGNESIUM

Three-quarters of the magnesium in our bodies is found together with calcium in our bones and teeth. Natural sources of magnesium are milk and dairy products, meat, nuts, cereals, and legumes.

average, less likely to suffer heart attacks than people living in soft-water areas. Some people take supplements to make sure they have enough magnesium in their body.

Chemical plants

Plants turn light energy from the Sun into chemical energy, in a process called photosynthesis. Without photosynthesis, there would be no plants or animals because animals, in order to live, need to eat either plants or other animals that themselves eat plants.

Photosynthesis only occurs because of the chemical action of a green pigment called chlorophyll, which plants have in their leaves. Chlorophyll is made mainly from carbon and hydrogen, but each molecule is held together by a single atom of magnesium at its center.

Periodic table

Everything in the universe is made from combinations of substances called elements. Elements are the building blocks of matter. They are made of tiny atoms, which are much too small to see.

The character of an atom depends on how many even tinier particles called protons there are in its center, or nucleus. An element's atomic number is the same as the number of protons.

Scientists have found around 110 different elements. About 90 elements occur naturally on Earth. The rest have been made in experiments.

All these elements are set out on a chart called the periodic table. This lists all the elements in order according to their atomic number.

The elements at the left of the table are metals. Those at the right are nonmetals. Between the metals and the nonmetals are the metalloids, which sometimes act like metals and sometimes like nonmetals.

- On the left of the table are the alkali metals. These elements have just one electron in their outer shells.
- On the right of the periodic table are the noble gases. These elements have full outer shells.
- Elements in the same group have the same number of electrons in their outer shells.
- Elements get more reactive as you go down a group.
- The number of electrons orbiting the nucleus increases down each group.
- The transition metals are in the middle of the table, between Groups II and III.

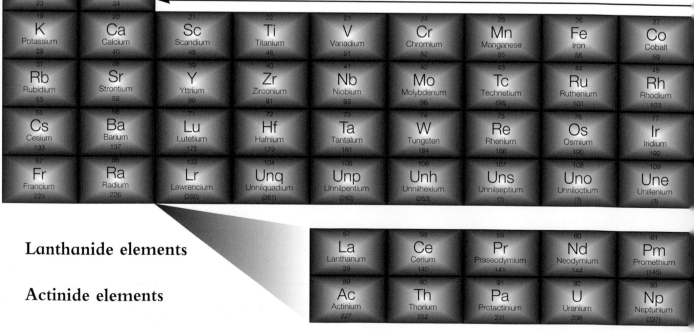

Group I	Group II	Transition metals						
1 H Hydrogen 1								
3 Li Lithium 7	4 Be Beryllium 9							
11 Na Sodium 23	12 Mg Magnesium 24							
19 K Potassium 39	20 Ca Calcium 40	21 Sc Scandium 45	22 Ti Titanium 48	23 V Vanadium 51	24 Cr Chromium 52	25 Mn Manganese 55	26 Fe Iron 56	27 Co Cobalt 59
37 Rb Rubidium 85	38 Sr Strontium 88	39 Y Yttrium 89	40 Zr Zirconium 91	41 Nb Niobium 93	42 Mo Molybdenum 96	43 Tc Technetium (98)	44 Ru Ruthenium 101	45 Rh Rhodium 103
55 Cs Cesium 133	56 Ba Barium 137	71 Lu Lutetium 175	72 Hf Hafnium 179	73 Ta Tantalum 181	74 W Tungsten 184	75 Re Rhenium 186	76 Os Osmium 190	77 Ir Iridium 192
87 Fr Francium 223	88 Ra Radium 226	103 Lr Lawrencium (260)	104 Unq Unnilquadium (261)	105 Unp Unnilpentium (262)	106 Unh Unnilhexium (263)	107 Uns Unnilseptium (?)	108 Uno Unniloctium (?)	109 Une Unnilennium (?)

Lanthanide elements	57 La Lanthanum 39	58 Ce Cerium 140	59 Pr Praseodymium 141	60 Nd Neodymium 144	61 Pm Promethium (145)
Actinide elements	89 Ac Actinium 227	90 Th Thorium 232	91 Pa Protactinium 231	92 U Uranium 238	93 Np Neptunium (237)

The horizontal rows are called periods. As you go across a period, the atomic number increases by one from each element to the next. The vertical columns are called groups. Elements get heavier as you go down a group. All the elements in a group have the same number of electrons in their outer shells. This means they react in similar ways.

The transition metals fall between Groups II and III. Their electron shells fill up in an unusual way. The lanthanide elements and the actinide elements are set apart from the main table to make it easier to read. All the lanthanide elements and the actinide elements are quite rare.

Magnesium in the table

Magnesium has atomic number 12, so it has 12 protons in its nucleus. It is positioned to the left of the table among the group of elements called alkaline-earth metals.

It is among the lightest of the metals, with an average atomic mass of 24.31. It is very reactive and easily forms compounds. It is mostly used in making various alloys.

Metals
Metalloids (semimetals)
Nonmetals

12 Mg Magnesium 24	
12	Atomic (proton) number
Mg	Symbol
Magnesium	Name
24	Atomic mass

			Group III	Group IV	Group V	Group VI	Group VII	Group VIII
								2 He Helium 4
			5 B Boron 11	6 C Carbon 12	7 N Nitrogen 14	8 O Oxygen 16	9 F Fluorine 19	10 Ne Neon 20
			13 Al Aluminum 27	14 Si Silicon 28	15 P Phosphorus 31	16 S Sulfur 32	17 Cl Chlorine 35	18 Ar Argon 40
28 Ni Nickel 59	29 Cu Copper 64	30 Zn Zinc 65	31 Ga Gallium 70	32 Ge Germanium 73	33 As Arsenic 75	34 Se Selenium 79	35 Br Bromine 80	36 Kr Krypton 84
46 Pd Palladium 106	47 Ag Silver 108	48 Cd Cadmium 112	49 In Indium 115	50 Sn Tin 119	51 Sb Antimony 122	52 Te Tellurium 128	53 I Iodine 127	54 Xe Xenon 131
78 Pt Platinum 195	79 Au Gold 197	80 Hg Mercury 201	81 Tl Thallium 204	82 Pb Lead 207	83 Bi Bismuth 209	84 Po Polonium (209)	85 At Astatine (210)	86 Rn Radon (222)

62 Sm Samarium 150	63 Eu Europium 152	64 Gd Gadolinium 157	65 Tb Terbium 159	66 Dy Dysprosium 163	67 Ho Holmium 165	68 Er Erbium 167	69 Tm Thulium 169	70 Yb Ytterbium 173
94 Pu Plutonium (244)	95 Am Americium (243)	96 Cm Curium (247)	97 Bk Berkelium (247)	98 Cf Californium (251)	99 Es Einsteinium [illegible]	100 Fm Fermium [illegible]	101 Md Mendelevium [illegible]	102 No Nobelium [illegible]

Chemical reactions

Chemical reactions are going on around us all the time. Some reactions involve just two substances; others many more. But whenever a reaction takes place, at least one substance is changed.

In a chemical reaction, the atoms stay the same. But they join up in different combinations to form new molecules.

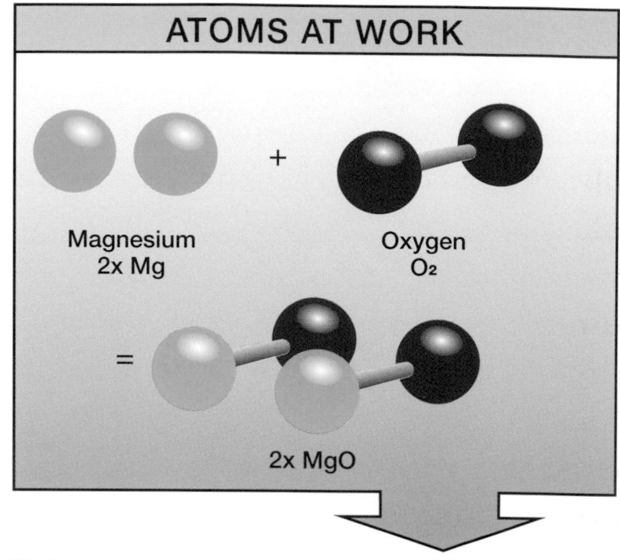

The reaction that takes place when magnesium reacts with oxygen can be written like this:

$$2Mg + O_2 \rightarrow 2MgO$$

Writing an equation

Chemical reactions can be described by writing down the atoms and molecules before and the atoms and molecules after. Since the atoms stay the same, the number of atoms before will be the same as the number of atoms after. Chemists write the reaction as an equation. This shows what happens in the chemical reaction.

These walls in Mexico are covered with stucco, which contains magnesium oxide.

Making it balance

When the numbers of each atom on both sides of the equation are equal, the equation is balanced. If the numbers are not equal, something is wrong. So the chemist adjusts the number of atoms involved until the equation does balance.

Glossary

alloy: A mixture of two or more metals.
aluminum: A metal that is often alloyed with magnesium.
asteroid belt: Hundreds of thousands of small pieces of rock that orbit in space, between Mars and Jupiter. They can cover an area many thousands of miles across.
atom: The smallest part of an element that has all the properties of that element. Each atom is less than a millionth of an inch in diameter.
atomic mass: The number of protons and neutrons in an atom.
atomic number: The number of protons in an atom.
bond: The attraction between two atoms that holds them together.
carbon fiber: A strong, lightweight material made from woven sheets of graphite set in resin.
casting: The process of pouring a molten metal into a mold, then letting it set to make an object.
chlorophyll: A green pigment in plants that converts light into chemical energy.
compound: A substance made of two or more elements that have combined together chemically.
corrosion: The eating away of a material by reaction with other chemicals, often oxygen and moisture in the air.
electrode: A material through which an electrical current flows into, or out of, a liquid electrolyte.
electrolysis: The use of electricity to change a substance chemically.
electrolyte: A liquid that electricity can flow through.
element: A substance that is made from only one type of atom. Magnesium is one of the elements that occur naturally.
ion: A particle of an element similar to an atom but carrying an additional negative or positive electrical charge.
metal: An element on the left-hand side of the periodic table.
ore: A collection of minerals from which metals, in particular, are usually extracted.
periodic table: A chart of all the chemical elements laid out in order of their atomic number.
photosynthesis: The process by which plants convert sunlight in chemical energy, releasing carbon dioxide and water vapor.
precipitate: A solid substance that drops out of a solution.
radioactivity: The sending out of particles from the center of an atom.
reactive element: An element that easily interacts with other elements.
talc: a mineral form of magnesium.
ultraviolet: A form of radiation similar to light but invisible to the naked eye.
uranium: A heavy, radioactive metal, used as fuel in nuclear power stations.

Index